Animal Food Chains

written by John Lockyer

A food chain shows us who eats what. Most food chains begin with green plants. Green plants make their own food from water, the sun and the dirt. This gives them energy to grow bigger and to grow leaves, flowers, fruit, or nuts.

grasshopper

plant

rat

food chain

lizard

rabbit

snake

eagle

Animals cannot make their own food. They must move around to find it. The food they eat gives them energy to grow, walk, run, fly, jump and think.

3

Some animals just eat plants. They are called herbivores. Elephants are herbivores. Some animals just eat meat. They are called carnivores. Lions are carnivores.

Some animals eat both plants and meat. They are called omnivores. Bears are omnivores. All animals are part of a food chain. This is how they stay alive.

elephant

Grass grows everywhere. Grasshoppers eat the grass. Rats eat the grasshoppers and snakes eat the rats. Small birds eat seeds and grasshoppers, while big birds eat rats and snakes.

Zebras, elephants and giraffes eat the grass too. They must take care because big cats like lions will eat them.

grasslands

The rainforest is a warm and wet place. Many trees in the rainforest grow fruit or nuts. Birds like to eat fruit and nuts. Monkeys like to eat them too, but they will eat little animals as well if they can catch them.

Monkeys must take care on the ground and in the trees, because of large snakes and big cats, who would eat them.

There is never enough food for animals that live in the desert. Insects eat any seeds they can find. Lizards and small birds eat the insects.

Small animals know they must take care around rocks because that's where snakes like to hide. Flying eagles are always on the lookout for birds, rabbits, snakes, and lizards to eat.

There are food chains in rivers and streams too. Water plants are food for bugs and shrimp. Small fish and small birds eat the bugs and shrimp. Ducks and birds with long legs eat the little fish.

Big fish eat almost everything that lives underwater. Big birds with big beaks eat the large fish.

freshwater

The food chain in the ocean has many plants and animals. Some of the small plants and animals are called plankton. Schools of small fish swim through the plankton with their mouths open so they can eat it.

Bigger fish eat the smaller fish. Sharks eat the bigger fish. Sharks must keep away from hungry orcas that hunt together.

People are part of many food chains.
These are some foods that people eat:
bread, eggs, milk, fish.
What is the food chain for each one?
Can you think of other food chains for people?